S0-ADW-377

The Sahara is Cold at Night

and Other Questions About Deserts

Jackie Gaff

KING*f*ISHER

NEW YORK

KINGFISHER
a Houghton Mifflin Company imprint
215 Park Avenue South
New York, New York 10003
www.houghtonmifflinbooks.com

First published in 2002
10 9 8 7 6 5 4 3 2

2TR/0602/TIM/HBM/128MA

Copyright © Kingfisher Publications Plc 2002

All rights reserved under International and
Pan-American Copyright Conventions

LIBRARY OF CONGRESS CATALOGING-IN-PUBLICATION DATA
has been applied for.

ISBN 0-7534-5434-3

Series designer: David West Children's Books
Author: Jackie Gaff
Consultant: Keith Lye
Illustrations: James Field (SGA) 5br, 8-9b, 22, 25tr,
    27tr, 30-31; Chris Forsey 10-11, 20, 21tl, 28-29;
    Mike Lacey (SGA) 4-5m, 9tr, 24m, 25b, 26;
    Mick Loakes 15bl; Steven Sweet 6-7, 24bl;
    David Wright 12-13, 14, 15tr, 15mr, 16-17,
    18-19, 21tr; Peter Wilkes (SGA) all cartoons.

Printed in China

CONTENTS

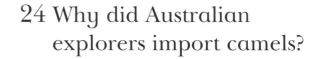
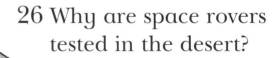

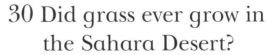

What is a desert?

Deserts are the driest parts of the world—places where it hardly ever rains. Most have less than 10 inches (25cm) of rain a year—a tenth of the rain that falls every year in rain forests, the wettest parts of the world.

● Deserts aren't just the world's driest places. They're also the windiest.

Are all deserts hot?

In many of the world's deserts it is hot enough during the day to fry an egg on a rock. Not all deserts are like this though. Some deserts have boiling hot summers and freezing cold winters, while others are chilly all year round.

● Even if you're going to a hot desert, remember to bring a sweater. Although daytime temperatures can reach over 104°F (40°C), it can drop to below 32°F (0°C) at night. Brrrrrr!

- When it does rain in the desert, it sometimes pours down. All of a desert's annual rain may fall in one tremendous storm lasting a few days.

- Even a sandy desert may be dotted with big rocks here and there. This huge boulder casts welcome shade during the hottest part of the day—time for people to shelter themselves from the Sun's sizzling heat.

Are all deserts sandy?

No—some are gravelly, while others are rocky or even snowy. Antarctica is a cold, snowy desert, for example, where there is no rain and little Sun.

- Some deserts are a cracked maze of dried-up salt flats, with a surface as hard as concrete.

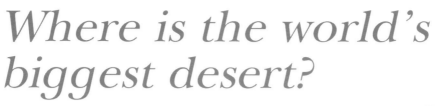

Where is the world's biggest desert?

The largest desert in the whole world is the Sahara in North Africa. It's larger than Australia and almost the size of the entire U.S.

- About one fifth of all the land on Earth is desert.

Map key

- The driest deserts where it hardly ever rains

- Deserts that have enough rain for some plants to grow

- Semideserts with enough rain for shrubs to grow

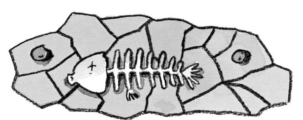

- At 282 ft. (86m) below sea level, Death Valley is the lowest desert (and place) in the U.S.

NORTH AMERICA

Great Basin

Mojave
Sonoran

Chihuahuan

ATLANTIC OCEAN

Equator

Peruvian

SOUTH AMERICA

Atacama

Patagonian

- South America's Atacama Desert is the world's driest place. Parts of the Atacama had no rain at all between 1570 and 1971—that's 401 years!

6

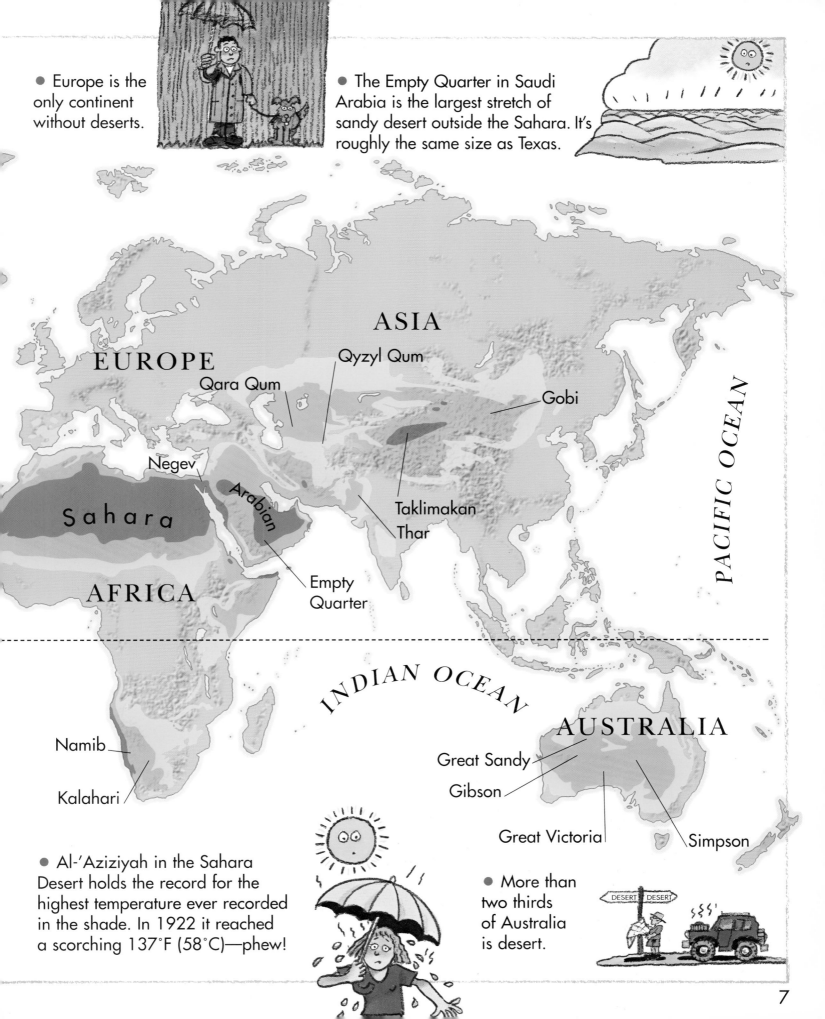

● Europe is the only continent without deserts.

● The Empty Quarter in Saudi Arabia is the largest stretch of sandy desert outside the Sahara. It's roughly the same size as Texas.

ASIA

EUROPE

Qyzyl Qum

Qara Qum

Gobi

Negev

Arabian

Sahara

Taklimakan

Thar

AFRICA

Empty Quarter

PACIFIC OCEAN

INDIAN OCEAN

AUSTRALIA

Namib

Great Sandy

Kalahari

Gibson

Great Victoria

Simpson

● Al-'Aziziyah in the Sahara Desert holds the record for the highest temperature ever recorded in the shade. In 1922 it reached a scorching 137°F (58°C)—phew!

● More than two thirds of Australia is desert.

Why are deserts sandy?

Sandy deserts are formed mainly by the wind. As it howls across the land the wind blasts at the rock, wearing it down. Slowly the rock cracks into stones and pebbles, which crumble into tiny grains of sand over time.

● Strong desert winds sometimes stir up huge clouds of sand. Wind-blown sand is powerful enough to strip the paint off a car.

How high are the tallest sand dunes?

Desert sand dunes come in many shapes and sizes, from camel-high bumps to steep-sided hills. The highest ones are over 985 feet (300m) tall—more than twice as high as Egypt's tallest pyramid!

Where can you find mushroom-shaped rocks?

In a desert of course! The wind carves rocks into all kinds of amazing and strange shapes when it howls away at them.

● At sunrise and sunset the rocks and sand of the Painted Desert in Arizona gleam a rainbow of colors—from blue and violet to gold, brown, and red.

● As the sand from a dune shifts and slips, it can make strange booming or singing noises—spooky!

● Some sand dunes look like a crescent moon . . .

● . . . while others are shaped like a star.

● An S-shaped sand dune is called a seif, from the Arabic word for sword.

What is an oasis?

Although very little rain falls in the desert, there are places where water rises to the surface from deep below the ground. When there's enough water all year round for plants to grow, we call that place an oasis.

● A qanat is a deep underground tunnel carved out by people to bring water into the desert.

When is there water in a wadi?

A wadi is a desert river valley, and most of the time it's as dry as a bone. When there's a rainstorm, however, the wadi fills up quickly, and for a while it becomes a roaring, raging torrent of water.

● Every year in the Australian desert town of Alice Springs people race up the dry bed of the Todd River, carrying bottomless boats!

How does sunlight trick desert travelers?

There's nothing a thirsty desert traveler wants to see more than water. But the shimmering blue pool on the desert surface isn't always water—it's just an image of the sky. These tricks of light are called mirages.

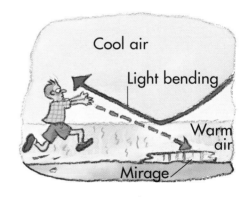

Cool air

Light bending

Warm air

Mirage

● A mirage happens when sunlight is bent as it travels through hot air near the ground. The scientific name for this bending is refraction.

How do plants survive in deserts?

All living things need water to survive, so coping with dry desert weather is tough for plants and animals. Plants slurp up water through their roots, and some desert plants have very long roots that extend deep down under the ground.

● The roots of the mesquite bush can reach water up to 98 ft. (30m) below the ground.

● When desert plants do get water, they hang on to it. Some use their leaves like a water tank, while cactuses store it in their fat, juicy stems.

Why are cactuses prickly?

A cactus' prickles are like a barbwire fence. They protect the plant and stop most animals from eating it.

When does the desert burst into bloom?

Some desert plants don't grow at all unless it rains. When there is a storm, the seeds sprout, grow, and bloom within a matter of weeks, turning the dusty desert into a colorful, flowering meadow.

● The tallest cactus is the giant saguaro. It can grow to a whopping 40 ft. (12m)—taller than four camels stacked up!

● The welwitschia of the Namib Desert looks more dead than alive. But don't be fooled. It can live for as long as 2,000 years.

● Instead of prickles, some cactuses are camouflaged to hide them from animals. Stone cactuses look exactly like pebbles.

How long can a camel last without water?

Camels can go for days without water—weeks if they find enough juicy plants to eat. When a camel gets a drink, it can gulp down 25 gallons (100*l*) in ten minutes.

● There are two kinds of camels. Arabian camels have one hump, while the Bactrian camels of Asia have two.

● A camel can go for weeks without food because its hump is like a backpack where food is stored as fat.

● Many desert lizards store fat in their tails.

Which desert animals never drink?

Jerboas (right) and kangaroo rats don't drink. They get all the water they need from plant seeds and other food.

● Foggy mornings give the darkling beetle of the Namib Desert all the water it needs. When it tips up its back, water droplets trickle down into its mouth.

Can toads live in the desert?

One kind of toad has a cunning way of surviving in the desert. For most of the year the spadefoot toad, found in the U.S., keeps its cool in a deep underground burrow. It only comes out to lay its eggs during the rainy season.

● Nearly all other toads live in wet, watery places because they're amphibians—animals that have to lay their eggs in water.

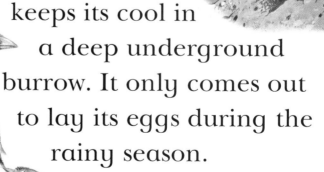

● The male sandgrouse is a flying water bottle. When it finds a puddle, it uses its fluffy breast feathers like a sponge, soaking up water to carry home to its chicks.

How do desert foxes keep their cool?

The kit fox's big ears work like radiators, giving off heat and cooling its body down. They also help it listen for enemies such as hyenas.

● The jackrabbit is another desert animal with big ears to help it keep cool.

Which animal has its own parasol?

Unlike most other small desert animals, ground squirrels spend their days out in the Sun. They find shelter from the afternoon heat under their own parasols—their tails!

● Many ground squirrels also use their tails for signaling each other if danger is near.

● The golden mole spends most of its life burrowing through the sand. It can tunnel over 2.5 miles (4km) in one night.

● Many desert animals have light-colored fur that helps keep them cool by reflecting sunlight.

● The elf owl finds shelter from the hot desert Sun in a hole in a tall saguaro cactus.

Why do desert animals love the dark?

It's a lot cooler out of the Sun than in it—many small desert animals find shelter from the daytime heat in underground burrows. They come out to hunt for food at night, or in the early morning or evening.

How do rattlesnakes kill their prey?

An attacking rattlesnake is lightning fast. It opens its mouth wide, swings its fangs forward, and then bites, injecting a deadly poison through them. Small victims die within seconds.

● Rattlesnakes are named for the rattling noise they make by shaking the tip of their tail.

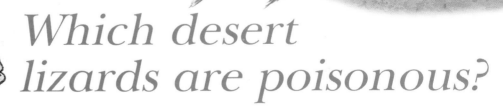

Which desert lizards are poisonous?

Hundreds of different lizards live in deserts, but only two are poisonous—the Gila monster of the U.S. and the beaded lizard of Mexico. But don't worry. These lizards mainly use their poison as protection against enemies, not to attack prey.

Why do scorpions have a stinger in their tail?

Scorpions inject poison through their tails, but only if they're really angry. Usually they use their claws to catch and kill prey. Scorpions have small eyes and can't see very well, so they track their prey using their senses of touch and smell instead.

● The chuckwalla lizard protects itself from its enemies by squeezing into a crack in a rock and puffing up with air. It's as hard to get out as pulling a cork from a bottle!

● Scorpions mainly eat insects and spiders, but large scorpions will eat lizards and mice.

How do people live in the desert?

Desert survival is all about finding enough water and food to stay alive. Some desert people move from place to place all the time, following good sources of water and food. These traveling people are called nomads.

● The San people of the Kalahari Desert are so good at tracking down water that they can find small pockets of it under the sand. They suck up the water through a reed straw and store it in an ostrich shell.

What do nomadic people find to eat?

Few desert nomads hunt for wild food these days. Instead most keep their own herds so they can drink the animals' milk or make it into cheese.

Who ate ants?

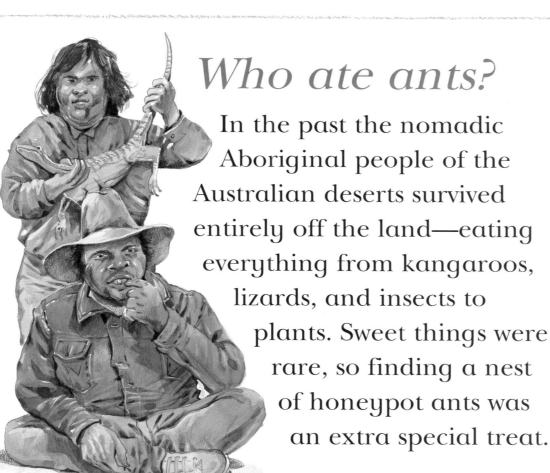

In the past the nomadic Aboriginal people of the Australian deserts survived entirely off the land—eating everything from kangaroos, lizards, and insects to plants. Sweet things were rare, so finding a nest of honeypot ants was an extra special treat.

● When rains make the desert bloom, honeypot ants feed on the sugary nectar of flowers. Some ants store the nectar in their bodies, turning themselves into living honey pots.

● The Tuareg are nomadic herders who live in the Sahara Desert. Their name means "the people of the veil"—the men's faces are almost completely hidden by their veillike turbans.

● Nomadic people do not travel every day—only when they need to refresh their water or food supplies.

Why do desert people build mud houses?

Mud is a fantastic building material. Homes with thick mud walls stay cool inside when the Sun is boiling hot outside and warm inside if the weather turns chilly. Best of all, mud is dirt cheap—you just have to dig it up.

● Homes can be built from layers of clay mud or from bricks made by mixing mud with straw or animal hair.

Are there towns in the desert?

There certainly are. Although thousands of desert people led nomadic lives in the past, not many do today. Most live around oases, or in river valleys such as the Nile, or on the desert fringe.

What is a yurt?

Travelers need portable homes, and yurts are the traditional round tents of the nomadic Mongol people of the Gobi Desert. They're made from wooden poles covered in felt made from sheeps' wool.

● The tents of the nomadic Bedouin people of the Middle East are covered in cloth woven from goats' hair.

Where do people paint with sand?

● In South America's Nazca Desert more than 1,200 years ago, people scratched huge pictures of birds and other animals into the stony ground.

The Navajo Indians create beautiful paintings with colored sand for use in healing rites and other traditional ceremonies. They live in the southeast of the Great Basin Desert in the U.S.

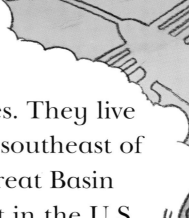

Why did Australian explorers import camels?

In February 1861 Robert Burke and William Wills became the first settlers to cross Australia from south to north. They wanted camels to carry their supplies because their route took them straight through the deserts in the continent's heart. But because camels aren't Australian animals, the explorers had to import them from Afghanistan.

Darwin

Burke and Wills die at Cooper Creek camp

Melbourne

• Sadly, Burke and Wills both starved to death on their return journey south. Their companion, John King, survived.

Who made it across the Sahara in an ultralight?

British explorer Christina Dodwell did in the 1980s during her mammoth 6,820-mile (11,000-km) flight across Africa. Her tiny flying machine was named *Pegasus*, after the winged horse in ancient Greek legend.

Which desert explorer carried water in his boots?

Sven Hedin of Sweden nearly died of thirst when he traveled across Asia's Taklimakan Desert in the 1890s. When he at last stumbled across water, two of his companions were dead, and the third had given up walking hours before. Hedin saved the third man's life by carrying water back to him in his boots.

● When Chinese monk Hsuan Tsang set off alone into the Gobi Desert in the 600s, almost the first thing he did was drop his water bag. He was saved by his horse, which smelled grass growing around a water hole and led him to safety.

Where do cars race across the desert?

The British racer Andy Green became the world's fastest person on wheels in October 1997 when his jet-propelled car, *Thrust SSC*, reached a mind-boggling 763 mph (1,228km/h). He set the record on the smooth, flat surface of Black Rock Desert in Nevada.

● Every January drivers race through the Sahara Desert during a rally from Paris, France, to Dakar, Senegal. In 1983, 40 drivers had to be rescued after losing their way in a sandstorm.

● The *Sojourner* rover was tested in U.S. deserts before its launch to Mars, where it landed in 1997.

Why are space rovers tested in the desert?

Being in a desert is the closest you can get on Earth to experiencing what it's like on Mars. And that makes a desert the ideal place for putting a space rover to the test.

Which is the world's hardest foot race?

You have to be made of steel to enter the Marathon of the Sands. This foot race takes place in the Sahara Desert with runners covering around 145 miles (230km) in six days—that's farther than five normal marathons!

• Although the temperature can reach 113°F (45°C) in the day, the Saharan runners have to carry food, clothes, and everything else they need—except a tent.

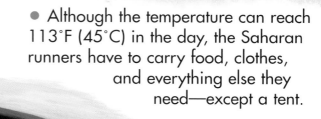

• Camels are raced like horses in the Arabian deserts. They can run faster than 20 mph (30km/h).

Is there treasure in the desert?

Yes—gold, silver, and diamonds have all been found in the desert. One of the world's largest diamond mines is in the Kalahari Desert in Africa.

- Salt was as precious as gold in ancient times—there were salt mines deep in the Sahara Desert.

What is black gold?

People often call oil "black gold," because it's one of our planet's most valuable natural resources. Finding it on their land has made individual people and entire countries very, very wealthy.

- Much of the world's oil is drilled from rocks beneath the deserts in the Arabian Peninsula.

● Treasure doesn't always glitter. In 1923, American archaeologists were the first to discover fossilized dinosaur eggs in the Gobi Desert. The eggs were later sold for thousands of dollars.

How can deserts give us clean energy?

Solar power plants are places where the Sun's heat is used to generate electricity. They're much cleaner than power plants that burn oil or coal, and hot deserts are the ideal places to build them.

● The world's largest solar power plant is located in the Mojave Desert in California.

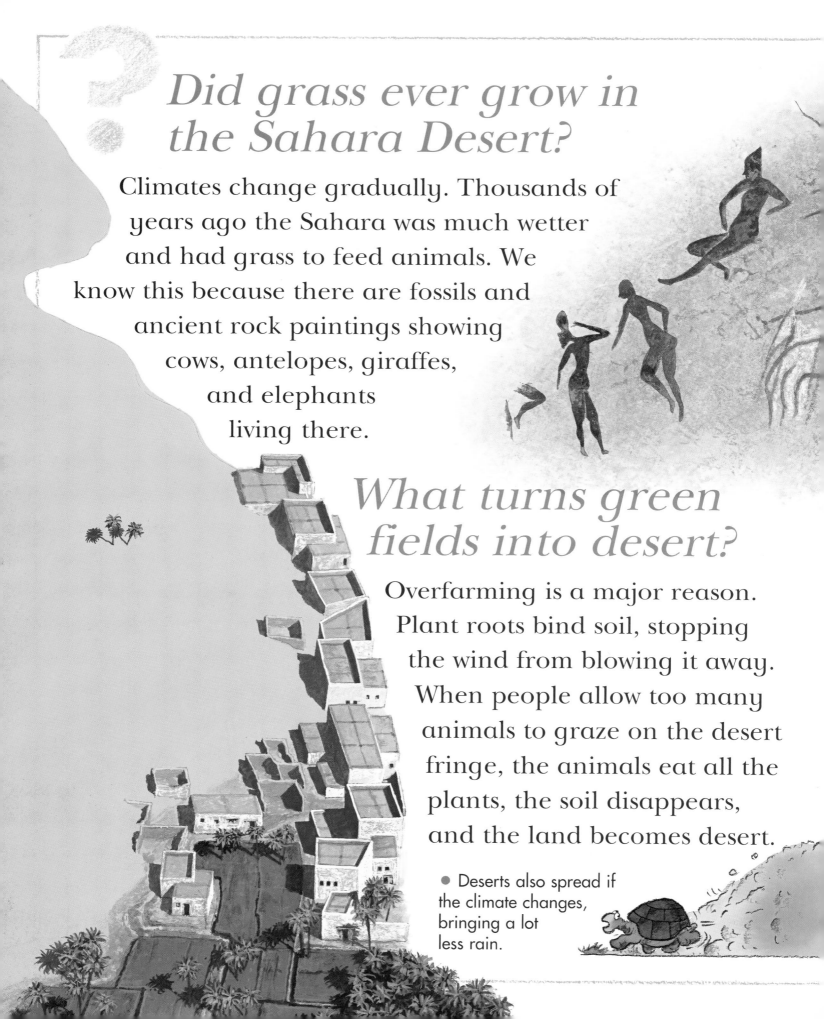

Did grass ever grow in the Sahara Desert?

Climates change gradually. Thousands of years ago the Sahara was much wetter and had grass to feed animals. We know this because there are fossils and ancient rock paintings showing cows, antelopes, giraffes, and elephants living there.

What turns green fields into desert?

Overfarming is a major reason. Plant roots bind soil, stopping the wind from blowing it away. When people allow too many animals to graze on the desert fringe, the animals eat all the plants, the soil disappears, and the land becomes desert.

● Deserts also spread if the climate changes, bringing a lot less rain.

● The rock paintings also show people swimming in ancient Saharan rivers and lakes, as well as water animals such as hippopotamuses and crocodiles.

Can deserts be changed into green fields?

Huge watering projects are one way of making deserts green again. In parts of North Africa the sand is dotted with round fields, created by gigantic spinning sprinklers.

● In some parts of Saudi Arabia, the leftovers from refined oil are sprayed on sand dunes. The gray, muddy mixture holds water, allowing plants to grow.

Index

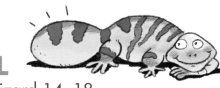